Trading In My Sorrows

Josie Dennison

Written by J. Dennison
www.jdennison.org

Published by Writers Block Publishing LLC
www.writersblockpublishingllc.com

Trading In My Sorrows

Introduction

Lord promises us songs for sorrows and Beauty for Ashes. For some of us, obtaining these promises are part of a long and rough journey. Because of who I am and what I've been through, I've learned there are different types of people in this world. Many people are misunderstood. Growing up, I always had a way of thinking. Sometimes it got me in trouble, and other times it's saved my life. I always thought that I was the black sheep of the family, but I was just different in reality. We were all forced to go to church, which I didn't mind until I got a little older and had questions.

Back then, the only answer was: "Because I said so."

That response would later change everything I thought I believed in. I was an honor student that brought home all kinds of rewards. I loved to write. I would write every chance I had. I was also very quiet growing up and did not have many friends, but I was popular because I got into many fights. Being dark-skinned was not cool back then, so I did not have to look for trouble; it often came to me. (But that's a whole different story). With that being said, I was full of rage and anger. If someone came to me with any kind of what I call Raw-Raw, I would unleash all that rage and anger on them; trust me, I had a lot of it. Because I was an honor roll student, I'd just got a call home and detention when I did get in trouble. Plus, English was my mother's

Josie Dennison

second language, so I was confident she would not care about what they would say to her (that is not the case anymore). I've been through many storms in my life, but I've also overcame many obstacles. As I look over my life, I can't help think through it all the Lord had a plan for my life. My name is Josie. This is my story...

Trading In My Sorrows

May 15, 2001

Dear Diary,

I'm so lost I don't understand how I got here, what I did to get here? Yet here I am, seventeen pregnant and married. Well, I guess I do understand how I got here. See, coming from my background and culture, you get pregnant, girl you getting married. I don't think my mom really understands the damage this cultural stuff can do. All I wanted to do was be a normal teenager, go to basketball games, go to the movies, and hang out with my friends at the mall. But no, I had to live my life as a sheltered Christian girl wearing skirts with tennis shoes and being bullied at school.

So I figured I'd break the mold; instead of going to prayer one night, I decided I was going to the football game, and that was all it took for mom to say no ma'am. Two grown-ups cannot live in the same house goodbye, so off I went to live with my sister. I still don't understand how a mother can put their child out over a basketball game if that's the God you serve telling you to do that, honey, you can have him. Everyone else got baptized, so I guess her plan for me was to get baptized too. No one ever told me why I needed to be baptized; all they told me is that after I got baptized, is that I would get seven more demons if I did something wrong. So why would I want to do this?

Josie Dennison

Whatever I guess, I'm not making heaven. I don't even want to go to this church; why can't we go somewhere we all understand what they are talking about or provided a translator. You get bullied in Sunday School more than a regular school. Plus, I always see the same people who got baptized skipping school and doing all this wild stuff. So what's the point of being baptized?

J.

Trading In My Sorrows

June 30, 2001

Dear Diary

I know it's been a minute since I spoke to you, so let me fill you in, girl. So I've been staying at my sister's house. Things going all right; however, there is way too much drama going on around here. So, this is supposed to be my sweet sixteen; some random guys from the neighborhood show up. I don't even know who they are or who invited them. My sweet sixteen wasn't what I expected it to be because I don't have that many friends, so the five people I do know came. That's nothing compared to what happened after the party.

Somehow, I was set up by someone on some robbery attempt. Mind you only place I've ever known was church and school. So I don't know the first thing about committing a robbery. The cops came, did their little investigation, chased me down, and took me to the police station for questioning. They had the nerve to ask me why I ran.

"Well, maybe because I have never seen a cop up close." I ran from the cops but eventually turned myself in. Anyhow, we got that all cleared up and found out that the person who claimed I robbed them had set themselves up to get robbed for insurance purposes; go figure.

Josie Dennison

I asked the cops to take me home to my mom's house. That was not a good outcome because Mom said No, not welcomed here.

Well, since she doesn't want me in her home and I have issues at the other one's house, I came to stay with John, his mother, and little brother. They are really cool, but I found out he is part of a gang. I feel like a little sister here; they took me in as if I was their own. Time to create a new family!

J.

Trading In My Sorrows

July 1, 2001

Dear Journal

I can't believe I found you! I've been looking all over for this one journal so I can continue writing. Girl, so much has happened; it's going to take a few pages to fill you in. So I'm no longer at John's house with his mom. I found my way. I've been going back and forth a lot with different friends. I also joined the crew. I'm officially a little sister. I thought it was going to be like the movies, and I had to do something crazy, but it was not. I just told them the truth about what was going on; that's it. As of right now, though, I'm staying with this old lady, I don't know her name, and I'm pretty sure she's doing witchcraft up in here. She's been summonsing all types of people. That's okay, though. I got my piece; let someone come mess with me.
I'm lightning folks up, and I mean everybody.

There was a curfew put out one night, and I call myself walking to the store. How about the cops picked me up and took me to some Juvenile Detention Center. I tried to explain to them I didn't know anything about no curfew,

"I don't watch the news."
They weren't hearing that, so they tried to take me to my mom's house. I try to tell the cop,

Josie Dennison

"You wasting your time,"
But I guess he had to see for himself. When we got there, she was like;
"I don't know her."
The cop looked at me. I looked at him and asked,
"Can I go now sir,"
He politely said sure. Right as I was about to leave, here comes Big Brother Super Saver.
"That's my sister."

I beg that man to take me back to The Detention Center, but he refused, so as soon as he left, I left too. I got me a little family. I'm good. Take me back to them, please. One phone call and they came in scoop me up like a real family do. They had Mom come checked me out of that Detention Center, who would have thought. I don't know how they did it, but they did it, and that same night I was out back home my home in my hood. A few nights later, I went to my first real party at the hotel where I met this white dude, (let's call him Mike in this book to save face). He kept asking me for my number, but I told him I don't talk to white boys. Well, I ended up giving him my number anyhow; I mean, what will it hurt?

I started talking to him; he seemed cool, but he's got a lot of baby mama drama. He showed me what weed was. That stuff will have you stuck like chuck. I been hanging with him a lot, and seems to want good things in life, but I don't know about all this relationship stuff. I'm cool, just hanging. We both started working at this

Trading In My Sorrows

car wash owned by his friend. I met his family; they seem cool but kind of mean to me, probably because I'm young. Makes no never mind to me; as long as no one runs up on me, I'm cool.

Oh, and I've been secretly talking to Mom. I don't know why it has to be a secret; maybe she doesn't want anyone to know that she keeps in touch with the devil, or maybe it's a Jesus thing, child but whatever. We talk every day now. I told her that Mike and I moved into a rooming house. She was not happy with that at all, but we can't get a real place yet. I think she likes the previous guy I was talking to better, but oh well.

J.

Josie Dennison

June 30, 2002

Dear Journal

I have so much to tell you. Oh My God, Life has just been everywhere. I was washing a car today and threw up all over it. I was so embarrassed because everyone was watching. I thought I was just sick come to find out I'm pregnant. Yes, I'm pregnant! I can't believe this. I'm going to have a baby.

The girl at the rooming house where we live has been trippin. She kept making threats. I told her after I drop his baby, I'm going to bust her lips open. She got mad and called the cops on me said I threatened her first. I told the cops;

"I'm pregnant; what am I going to do to her." She kept going on and on about how I am a minor, and she doesn't play with little girls. Okay, this little girl got a big fist; try me if you want to. The cops played into her cry baby self and started focusing on me being a minor, so they asked to call my mom. I lied and told them I don't know where she's at, so leave me alone. She has denied me at every encounter what is going to be different now. It's clear; she doesn't love me. I've seen kids do some off the wall stuff, and their mom still come running.

Trading In My Sorrows

The police left, and I told that lady she was going to pay as soon as I dropped this load. A few days later, private investigators came knocking on my door, and they were talking crazy stuff about child rape. Come to find out, my neighbor reported that Mike kidnaped me and was holding me hostage.

"Right!!" I told her. "Girl, I know you serve a might God because he is saving you right now from this molly woop I have for you!"

Well, because of her report, my mom had to get involved. So they went to my mom and asked if she knew I was with this older man and pregnant. She didn't respond (probably cause she knew before anyone else did); instead, she turned the tables on them. She told them Mike would marry me. I'm like, wait a minute, who said anything about marriage. Mom came to Mike and me and told us we were to get married, or she would sign these papers for the investigators to put him in jail for statutory rape. From there we started planning a wedding.

That investigator kept coming back, asking my mom just to sign the papers and not allow us to get married. She claimed that Mike had a record for beating on women in the past. I don't believe that, but I also don't want to get married. It's too late for that now. I don't want him to go to jail for rape when that is a lie. Everywhere we went, everyone was saying the same thing about Mike. Mind you; I've never met his peoples until now.

Josie Dennison

Mom took us to court and signed some paper that signed over a minor, so the wedding is on. At first, I didn't want to get married, but this is kind of cool to get all dressed up and stuff (lol). I think that's the only part I like about it. My best friends' mom came to talk to my mom and asked her not to allow me to get married. Being pregnant does not make this any easier all I do is cry. I don't feel like writing anymore. I'll talk to you once all of this is over.

J.

Trading In My Sorrows

July 14, 2002

Dear Journal

I'm married now. I think I actually like it. It's not as bad as I imagined. I was thinking about something today, Mike and I got married back in July; I can only thank God for this. God, I guess I can do this after all.

Everything tried to stop it from happening; children and families got involved. At some point, Mike didn't want to get married either. He was just going to take the jail sentence and fight it. My mom almost gave up, but by that time, it was too late. Everything was paid for. In the midst of it all, Mike went to jail for confronting that crazy neighbor girl that started all this. This has all been a big mess, but if it makes Mom happy, fine whatever, I'll be the best wife I can be whatever that means, time to start embracing this married thing.

Josie
&
Mike
4-life

Josie Dennison

July 15, 2002

Dear Journal

I'll get straight to the point. I want to get out of this house and get a place with just Mike and me. This man is supposed to be helping us out, but I don't want to be here. I don't see Mike and me staying here and letting someone use us. I hope the Lord helps us find a place soon.

Mike has to pay for some of the things this dude needs plus $200 a month to sleep on the floor in the living room.

That's the last time we pay for the next man's food or anything.

But anyhow, I can't wait to leave this place and have my own. I plan to go to school in the morning and Mike will go to work that way things will be alright until I have my baby, which we still have not bought anything for.

J.

Trading In My Sorrows

July 19, 2002

Dear Journal

I need to start going back to school next week, or they are going to kick me out. I also really need a job. I don't have any money to even get to school. I need to finish school before my baby gets here. We need to come up with $600 to move. Lord, I ask that you please help us and give me the strength to do what I have to do. I hate my life, but I can't wait to meet my baby.

"You hear that, MY BABY."
If it weren't for this baby, I just off myself, but now I can't, well I don't want to. I'm going to be the best mom and fight for mines.

J.

Josie Dennison

July 22, 2002

Dear Journal

What's up! Well, today, I was so proud of myself. I got out of bed and went to school. You know how long I've been saying I want to go and try to finish school. Well, today, I made my first move. I pray that God helps me please because I had a nice day at school.

On the way home, I stopped by the car wash to talk to my friend Gloria for a bit. It's okay, though; I've been through much worse. Now I just hope I can find a good job or some positive way to make money for my baby and me; we'll be straight. I'll pray for God to help us.

J.

Trading In My Sorrows

July 23, 2002

Dear God,

I want to finish school, have my baby, give my baby everything he or she needs, and, most importantly, I need another job that's not too hard. I want to be a very calm person, so even when things are not going right, I don't get all worked up and raise my blood pressure. This is my first baby, and there is nothing more important to me, not school, work, a house, or a dude. I don't want anything to be wrong with my child, so I'm going to stop stressing and start ignoring things that hurt me. Things like what people say and how they act, like they don't understand what's going on. If anything happens to my baby because of me, I don't think I can live with that. So I'm going to just chill, Ill deal with these people once I drop. This baby is the only thing that matters in life right now. I don't care if I have to walk the streets with it as long as he/she is with me. I'll be fine.

J.

Josie Dennison

August 8, 2002

Dear Journal

There are somethings a person says to you that you just can't let go. Like that time, my mom told the cops I wasn't her child. When I have my baby, there is nothing he/she can do to make me say that. But, I never thought Mike would make it on that list as well.
He said to me,

"I know that you are a hoe and that you were probably out there tricking too, and I know you want to go back."
"First of all, dude, when you met me, my hustle game was strong. Never had to spread my legs for a dollar; granted, I did a lot of crazy stuff but never that."

I should have just robbed him and called it a day. I would not have been in this mess with a baby on the way. But he such a cry baby we would have had to lay him out.

I should have never given in to any of this and stayed on the block with my real family. I'll never forget or forgive them for saying that. I promise you he will eat his words, oh sucker duck self. I'm the fool to get pregnant by this wanna-be hustler, this bottom feeder dude. Anyhow, just breathe, think about the baby.

J.

Trading In My Sorrows

August 9, 2002

Dear Journal

Being married is not what I thought it was going to be. It's boring. I thought that you can have your man all to yourself with no problems and no worries while still having fun. On Friday nights we can go somewhere like a bayside, the movies, the beach or somewhere anywhere, as long as it's not the club. We could even stay home on Saturday nights and watched a movie until we fall asleep, and Sunday morning, we can clean up and just chill.

Oh well

Well, I'm eight months pregnant now, and yes, I'll be having a BOY!! I have a godmother for him already but no godfather. I'll think of someone soon. I need some more things for him. I'm hoping to get them soon. I'm kind of scared with my due date getting close, but besides that, I think I'm ready and waiting.

J.

Josie Dennison

November 13, 2002

Dear Journal

Finally, settled into my new place. Today, we ate Chinese food and watched a movie, and I fell asleep for about an hour. I woke up, and we put Christmas lights up and listens to Christmas music. I took a shower we enjoyed each other's company for the rest of the day. The sad part is these days are very few, so I have to write about them. I might be the only person on earth who gets excited about sitting around doing nothing fancy, but my mind is at peace today, and I have to enjoy it without wondering why.

J.

Trading In My Sorrows

November 15, 2002

Dear Journal

Today was okay. I talked to my best friend from school, some other friends and my big sister. My big sister is in town, I want to see her, but it's not a good idea. We are so cool, but together we create mayhem.

I found a girl's number in Mike's pocket. He tried to hide and say it was for one of his friends. At this point, I don't care anymore. I have better things to worry about, like my baby boy. I'm just worried because I'm not mad like I use to get. Seems like the more stupid stuff he does, the more don't care. I hope that does not mean I'm starting not to care about him. When you don't care about someone, you have no love for them. At this point, I do love him hope he does not mess that up.

J.

Josie Dennison

November 16, 2002

Dear Journal

Today was a good day. We went to the flea market USA and Liberty. I had $50, so I brought him two CDs out of the kindness of my heart, and I bought my son a first day home outfit. We ate and came home.

It started raining for the rest of the night. We started cleaning up together, but he fell asleep, so I did the rest. After I took a shower, I lay down, and we started talking and making plans for the baby to come.

Something felt weird, like I could not even sit down right, and I was hurting like crazy. I'm going to sleep before I start crying again.

J.

Trading In My Sorrows

November 17, 2002

Dear Journal

Today was a good day. My mother came by, and she brought me some food from rice and fish and beans. That was a shocker! I cleaned up, took a shower, ate, and laid down for the rest of the day. Then Mike came home. I was so happy to see him because all I could think about was this pain all day.

At one point, I started crying when Mike saw that I was crying, he asked what was wrong. I didn't want to tell them because I was so embarrassed, but eventually, I did. He took me to the hospital; they checked me out, gave Mike some medicine for me, and I was even more embarrassed. I never knew what a hemorrhoid was until today. Apparently, most pregnant women get them, especially at the end of pregnancy, because the baby is so big.

So I thank God that that's over with. I have to see a doctor in Hialeah. I guess he's going to deliver my baby. I think that day is closer than it seems. Just get this boy out of me. He driving me crazy now.

J.

Josie Dennison

November 19, 2002

Dear Journal

Today was a good day, as well. I woke up early and went to the Hialeah Hospital; I almost passed out on the bus stop. When I got there, they told me exactly what I thought they would. I was already registered at Jackson, so I have to stay there. I guess I'm going to deliver my baby at Jackson North. I'm so happy that there's only a couple of days left, 24 days to be exact. I can't wait to have my baby lying in bed next to me. I'm so excited. Anyways I got some medicine for my so-called bump. Mike has been a good help to me. He helps me with applying to medicine without complaining.

Right now, he's showing much love in little ways. At night, he tries to hold me and rub my back. We started walking places together until baby Damien gets here. I'm not sure about his name just yet, but I like that name. We shall see, won't we? Haha.

J.

Trading In My Sorrows

November 22, 2002

Dear Journal

Today was only a good day because I woke up and did exactly what I said I was going to do. Think I need the Bible because just when things are going well with Mike and me, he gives me something to doubt him about again. He calls himself going on a fishing trip with some dude that we hardly know. So he won't be home for two days. The problem is not the fishing trip. The problem is, I don't believe a word Mike says or the so-called friend. He took all his nice clothes, nice shoes, even took some cologne; before they left, I offered them some condoms because let's be for real. You're going on a fishing trip looking like Pimp Chronicles. They think I didn't see the condom set that dude had, but I did.

He never walks around with condoms. I can tell that I'm starting not to care for Mike as much as I used to. I have to keep my guard up with him; it's a shame. All I want is my baby to come so I can have someone to hold, love, and who wants my love.

Oh, and another thing is, see everything he is doing to me now; I'm going to make sure he feels me once I have this baby and get back in shape. I don't think it's fair that I have to sit home waiting to have his baby, and

Josie Dennison

he just runs around the streets. There's nothing anyone can say or do to prove to me that Mike is not cheating. I know I don't deserve this. I didn't do anything wrong to him, but that's okay. I hope God sees what's going on, but they aren't going to tell me the truth. They just laugh at me; well, when I get back to the way I was before, I want to see who's going to be laughing. I'm not going to cheat, but he is going to feel me. After all, I am 17 years old. I can pop right back. He should be trying to hold on to me.

J.

Trading In My Sorrows

November 23, 2002

Dear Journal

Today was a good day. I woke up, ate some noodles, and drank some water down soda. Well, Mike call and I didn't want to talk to him because he left me here by myself and the way I was feeling yesterday I really don't want to talk to him. But I went ahead and talk to him anyway.

I was so mad yesterday that I cried. And I made sure I let him know about that. He said that he missed me and he wanted to come home, but he has to wait for his friend. He also claimed that he did not know that he would miss me as much because it was only for two days. What a nice thing to say, right?

He claimed that he would never leave me again. I hope he's not lying. Perhaps I was wrong yesterday, but I doubt that very much. I might take him up on his offer and take this check and finish school while I work. He said I still have a chance, and I can't wait until he comes home so we can discuss this.

J.

Josie Dennison

December 28, 2002

Dear Journal

What's up? Today calls for celebration as of today, we mark one year that Mike and I have been together he probably doesn't remember, but I'll ask him to make me breakfast this morning.

Trading In My Sorrows

December 15, 2002

Dear Journal

My son was born, and it was crazy. My water broke at home, but I refuse to go to the hospital cause I been going there a lot only to be sent home to walk. Well, I finally went when I could not take it anymore. They gave me a shot in my back. But the most amazing part is my mom showed up; I was in pain until I saw her face like say what she came. She was so grossed out she could not stay in the room. But I requested that she cut the cord, and she did. I'll never forget this day.

J.

Josie Dennison

January 1, 2003

Dear Journal

Happy New Year today is a new year. I thank God that I'm still alive and breathing, and thank God my son is with me. Other than that, I'm having the worst day of my life. I welcomed in the New Year with my husband beating on me because I would not let him sleep with my friend, and that's when all the truth came out. He called all his side chicks, main chicks and asked them could he go live with them. He told me he doesn't give an F- about me. I can take my baby and go.

I thought I had my husband to count on, to love me, and I love him, but I guess not. You don't love me. You married me so you can get away from the police, and that case that was pending as soon as I turned 18, the plan was to leave me. But I have my son Damien now, and I love him very much, and I pray that my son and I will be very close. I think Mike has me here as a placeholder for when he finds his true love.

I just really want to be happy. I want to know what I have done to deserve all that's going on in my life. I don't cheat. I don't talk to anyone else but my husband; I just wanted to have him to myself, but I guess that failed. I did my best to be a good wife and friend. I don't know

Trading In My Sorrows

what to do anymore; it's a shame that I'm afraid of my husband. It is hard for me even to trust

Josie Dennison

February 16, 2003

Dear Journal

What's up! I know I haven't wrote in you in a very long time, but the reason for that is because I've been working and keeping the baby. When I come home from work, I be so darn tired.

Today, I went to work, but they did not have any work for me, but tomorrow they will. Mike still asks this old girlfriend for money, but that's his problem. I don't care anymore. I don't know what he does behind my back while I'm at work. But I don't care anyway. Whatever that's his problem and more power to him. Good luck; just hope you don't let a good thing go to waste.

Trading In My Sorrows

February 27, 2003

Dear Journal

Every man I'm surrounded by cheats.
After what I saw today, I don't trust no man; even the ones that I thought would never cheat. Every man I'm surrounded by cheats I sit here and watch them too, but they don't tell me when Mike cheats, so should I tell their wives. I found out today that even the holy of holy men cheat. Apparently, Mike is the leader of all the cheaters in his circle.

I'm not sure if the other women know at least I'm informed about my cheater. And these are women who are making good money, and you go to their houses, and everything is all fancy, and here they come to our little place and set up ways to cheat, I like I said at least I'm informed about my cheater.

In a way, I feel bad, but I can't tell them to stop because they all knew each other before I came around, and they are family. In a way, I cannot feel like I'm following my mother's footsteps, which I am not going to do. She had her first child at 18, so did I. She got married at 18, so was I. I may have got married a little younger, but still, I was married at the age of 18. Last but not least, she married a hoe, so did I. Mike claim he's changed, but I don't want to give in, and

Josie Dennison

then at the end, I look like a fool because that's what all those other ladies are looking like right now.

Mike lies so much I don't know when he's telling the truth. I don't know what to believe. Oh well, there is a God, and God is good; he sees everything I ain't doing anything wrong if he is, then at the end of the day, you are looking like a fool. I'll be the winner, and I don't think any other female is going to put up with Mike the way I do.

J.

Trading In My Sorrows

March 4, 2003

Dear Journal

Today was a good day because my son and I woke up and saw a new day, but one thing that has not changed is Mike is out for himself as always. Since Monday, he knew that on Wednesday I have to take a test to start school, and wednesday is the next day he called some lady and told her that he would do a $30 job for her. He knew that I was going to have to look after the baby, so he tells me don't go because he is not looking after the baby go sign up at Miami Dade, but if I said I got to go to work, everything will be okay.

See, you don't get paid for going to school. He said it's not his fault I dropped out of school for him to be my husband, and say something like that is wild to me. He's supposed to love me. All he does is put me down; just the other day, he said that I was a hoe and that I was tricking; that is a lovely thing to tell your wife especially knowing that it's not true, just anything to put me down. My truth, I never say anything about him, not knowing how to read or how he was a junkie war or about his mother being a junkie. Anyhow, I put myself here, so I'm going to deal with it, and I bet you I go back to school.

J.

Josie Dennison

March 11, 2003

Dear Journal

Today was a great day. I woke up happy, and so does my little family. I went and found out that I would take the test on April 10th and 11th; the test is 3 hours each day. That's just for me to enroll in the Technology School. I'm also going to take my driving test next week. I hope that I passed. I need to pray. God knows that I need to pass all these tests. It's the beginning of my life. I have to show my son something else; I can't be living off this dope money and SSI. Like what is that? My son will not be like these folks around here over my dead body.

J.

Trading In My Sorrows

March 13, 2003

Dear Journal,

It's starting all over again, Mike going out and coming home late. You know how girls get that gut feeling when your man is cheating on you. Well, that's how I'm feeling right now... I need to pass this test and get my life together quickly. Because if I find out that Mike is cheating on me, I'm going to leave him. I love him with all my heart, but I love myself more. I wanted to be married to a man who loves me and wants to be with me, a man who wants to be together all the time and do fun stuff together. I thought that's who Mike was. I know I was wrong. The only place we go together is the flea market; other than that, he gets all fresh to go to the night clubs alone. When we out, he looks like the next bomb, always wanting sex. I know I'm a good woman; I guess he does not see that. I'm always having these same feelings, but oh well, I don't think he'll ever change.

J.

Josie Dennison

March 27, 2003

Dear Journal

What's up? I know I haven't written in a long time, that's because I've been so busy. I got a job at McDonald's. I started a month ago. I'm working the night shift. Damion is 5 months now. He's chunky and cuter than ever. Now my mother thinks I have a sorry husband and a sorry job. She didn't think that when she made me marry him, lol. Anyhow, I got a car now. I'm still learning how to drive through. I know this was a quick entry; I just didn't want you to think I forgot about you. You still my A1. Good night

J.

Trading In My Sorrows

June 4, 2003

Dear Journal

I've decided to start saving money because I have some bad dreams. Last night I dreamed that Mike came and got me from work. When I got in the car, there were many bags with new stuff in them for him. When I asked him how he got the money for all this stuff, he told me his new girlfriend got it for him. I just started crying when we got home. I packed Damion's stuff and left to a big house. My baby was crying for his daddy, and I told him we're going to find him a new dad. Everyone asked me not to leave, but I just gave him the address to see his son. When I saw the girl, I pinned her down and beat the crap out of her real bad. Some lady dressed in all white called me to her porch and told me I couldn't leave him because that's where I was placed, and if I leave him, his life would be messed up, and it would be my fault. I told her the house I'm moving to was nice and pretty. She said, don't leave the house; just invite him in. The next day he came, I let him in, and he said he was sorry he wants to work things out and get back together. I told him, okay but not for me for the old lady dressed in white. But it felt like I did not love him anymore; I was just there. Then I woke up

J.

Josie Dennison

June 29, 2003

Dear God

Things are really bad right now. All Mike wants is sex and money, like get a darn job dude, or go sell some more crack. We never go anywhere together and never do anything together. He always gets what he wants, but when it comes to me, you can forget about it. Every time I get paid, he wants something, and I never have enough money to do anything for myself. I've been working for 2 months now, and I have nothing but a car. He makes debts, and I have to pay them every paycheck. It's like I'm working for him. When he doesn't get sex, he gets mad and says he'll get it from somewhere else. Well bye, dude, just leave me and my son alone. If I can't get what I want, why should he get me and my body?

I'm starting not to care anymore. I just want to go to the mall, the movies sometimes and places I've never been with, but I want to go with my son. He's always out with his brother-in-law and everyone else. I want flowers and a clean house sometimes. I promise he's only out for himself. I'm 18 now. I stayed because I thought he had had some good in him; he was going to change and treat me right. I do love him, but I believe that he is with me just to be with me. He talks to me in any kind of way. I have to beg him to do anything for

Trading In My Sorrows

me. If he was not getting anything from my check, I don't think he would even take me to work. Yet he

J.

Josie Dennison

August 15, 2003

Dear Journal

This marriage is stupid. This dude would rather be out anywhere with everyone except me. Now he claims he is out dealing drugs in a different county. He ain't never got no money when does he have money? I don't see a dime of it. He claims he is working for some girl and had her phone. What kind or of drug dealer are you? Like I always said, a bottom feeder. Here comes the Cut-off Dude; when you ready to be married and take care of your son, come see me. I don't know why I expect anything more from him.

J.

Trading In My Sorrows

September 8, 2003

Dear Journal

Since the last time I wrote, Mike and I have been talking about this so-called marriage, and things have been going very good. He started staying home more. He asked me to smoke with him, so I did. I'm not a fan of weed, by the way; that stuff makes you feel like a hunger fool. People be talking, and all I can do is smile and respond, yeah. Then everyone, like roaches, looking for food. Anyhow, things are good. I don't know if it's because we're high all the time, but I'll take it over the drama. Oh, by the way, I took that final test for my high school diploma. I pray to God I pass.

J.

Josie Dennison

September 21, 2003

Dear Journal

Things are still going well—time to start backing off of these so-called friends; they in too deep. I don't do well with the whole best friend thing; please back up you over here too much now. Well, in other news, Damion is 9 months now!! He learned how to say bye-bye. He's super healthy, and I thank God for that.
Damion
9 months old
My baby boy

J.

Trading In My Sorrows

November 2, 2003

Dear Journal

Things are not going so great anymore. I'm getting very tired of him asking me for money for stupid stuff and that darn car of his. When I don t give it to him, he'll get it from some other girl. I know I kept saying I'm starting not to care anymore; well, I finally reached that point. I wish he would just leave; I will be alright. He can go be the best hoe he wants to be. See, I've already worked everything out, so I can be happy with or without him. My son and I will be good.

J.

Josie Dennison

November 15, 2003

Dear Journal

I move to Gainesville, just Damion and me. Mike is supposed to be coming too soon just to see what's up. There was so much going on. I just could not stay any longer, so when my big sister offered me to come here, I did not hesitate. Plus, I feel like Mike does what he does because he knows I have no family where we live. We will see how things go here. I'm excited, but I don't want to stay here long because I so use to having my place.

J.

Trading In My Sorrows

Dear Journal

January 15, 2004

I got my place now only took a month. Mike comes and goes between here and Miami, so it's just me and bad butt Damion. This boy is so bad it don't make no sine he's only one year old. I braided his hair up and got his locks started. Sometimes I do miss Mike, but we are making it well up here, and I'm starting to learn my way around. Mike will be back after a few months, though. My sister and I are back to not talking again; truthfully, I don't even know why. But eventually, we'll be cool again. I asked him to separate, but he keeps saying we can work this out okay, we shall see, but for now, I'm okay.

J.

Josie Dennison

March 27, 2004

Dear Journal

Guess what Mike left, and he's been gone for a month now. Some girl named Monique has been calling my phone and telling me how she and Mike are supposed to be together. We just been talking; she been telling me so much stuff that I did not know. This has been going on for a while now. I find it funny how Mike told her all about me, yet she still trying to fight for their relationship. Man, I'm 19 years old trust and believe I don't deserve this crap here. I have never done anything to harm anyone, yet here I am going through this with this dude. I tried my best to make this man happy; I even do a thing that I don't want to do. I know I did too much for him and still got nowhere. All he ever did was give me ultimatums like if I don't do

Trading In My Sorrows

something, he'll leave me. To think I was so happy today now, I feel like under someone's shoe. Maybe I should feel like that because I take way too much, and that's why people treat me the way they do. I tried to move and see if things would get better, and they are getting worst. It's as if everyone waited for me to leave to come out of the woodworks. Lord, this is too much for me.

J.

Josie Dennison

April 2, 2004

Dear Journal

Well, Mike is here now, and he's asking me to move back to Miami. Truthfully I've been thinking about it, but I know what I'm going back to. Plus, he still ain't treating me like he's supposed to. Gainesville is so easy for Damion and me. Mike's sister keeps sending him money. Plus, he's getting his own money, so for me, this is good. My rent is low, and if I'm getting a job soon. I don't think Miami is for us. Soon as I go back and I find out about anything else, I'm going to be trying to leave again.

You ever love someone so much you'll do anything for them, but that person just keeps doing you wrong. That person keeps cheating and hoeing around. The funny thing is, he knows how it feels because he's been through that in his past, or so he says. I want him to know how that feels again; I just don't have it in me to do it. He claims I have bad ways, okay I can work on me, but what about you. What about my son.

J.

Trading In My Sorrows

April 13, 2004

Dear Journal

Well, today I got a job. Kim is in jail, but that's not my fault. My so-called husband is so worried about Kim being in jail and not the fact that she assaulted me at my house in front of my son. So yes, I beat her down, and I held her until the cops came inside. He keeps saying jail is not the place for anyone okay and. This girl came to my house with a knife. That's why she is in jail. I had a feeling they had something more going on. I walked into her on top of him one-day having sex. So yes, I waited till he went back to Miami and dragged her; there was blood everywhere.

I ripped the chin ring right out of her face. She got all that mouth and no hands and sleeping with people's husbands. The cops came and said they were going to charge me because I cause too much damage. Mind you, this fight started at my friend's house and ended up outside. The cops took her way because she had nowhere to go. I was busy trying to find someone to get my son. I come back inside my house and who's banging on my back door with a knife Kim, so I let her in. She obviously wanted some more. She knew the cops were outside processing me. The lady cop heard something going on inside, so she came in, and I told her y'all took her away; she came back with a knife. So yeah, they no longer charged me and took her to jail. Bet she won't be on top of nobody's man no more. But my husband is worried about her. Her own family ain't worried about her. That girl could have stabbed me. He more worried

Josie Dennison

about her. I'm not dropping no charges point blank period. Little does he know he's now a wanted fugitive because of whatever Kim told the cops. He claims he was helping her because she was homeless and bought this girl to my house. Maybe if I was hoe poppen p***y on the handstand, he would love me and care for me. Well, buddy, I'm not about to go that route to please no man, married or not. He knows I'm not going anywhere, so he can go live his life in Miami and have me here in Gainesville. When the other women are done with him, he comes back to me; the dummy. Whatever happens from here, only the Lord knows I tried for 3 years I'm completely turning my thought process now. Nothing tops knowing you side chick pulled out a knife on your wife, and you trying to save the side chick. Just leave already.

J.

Trading In My Sorrows

April 16, 2004

Dear Journal

After today I'll be single again. This dude still talking about Kim, so I told him: "Please go and be with Kim. You obviously want her." As a matter of fact, he can now be with Kim, Ronnie, Kema, and Monique. He wonders why we don't have sex more because I value my life. It's a wonder I ain't catch something by now. This dude even asked me to let Kim come stay with me and tried to convince me that I'm wrong. I have every intention to call one of my homies to come take permanent care of this whole situation. I promise they would be on the first thing moving to come handle this dude. When a dude starts giving you the third degree because of what you won't do for his side chick, what the ____ do I look like. You fill in the blank. Dude, get out my house now.

J.

Josie Dennison

Dear Journal

April 19, 2004

It's been a while, but I'm doing good now. Mike still being Mike; now he hanging around, but he's hanging with some new chick that claims to be a Bulldager, but her sister is in love with Mike. She came up to me and asked me if she could sleep with him. Y'all been doing this without my permission, so why ask now? Plus, what kind of stuff they got going on around here, I should have dragged her up and down the street, but I almost lost my son the last time I got into it with that Kim girl. He is hanging around back with these dudes that are always plotting to do him in oh well, not my business. I have a feeling they know the type of guy he is, so they using these girls to set him up. But who am I to say anything? I'm just going to sit back and watch because baby, this is going to be good.

J.

Trading In My Sorrows

April 29, 2004

Dear Journal

Hahaha guess who is in jail because he got set up Mike, of course. Now I'm his amazing wife; he keeps writing me letters.

Dear Josie.
By the time this letter reaches your hand, it would find you and my kid in the best of health and in high spirits. I wanted to tell you happy late birthday. I'm sorry that I'm not home to celebrate with you. I've been walking around wondering why you haven't called or visited me. I wonder if you still love me even though baby I know that I broke the rules by hanging out with those guys eating crabs.
I wish that I would have listened to you. Now that I'm in here, I feel like a failure because my intentions were to come here and make a better life for you and my kid. Hope that you are not giving up on me because I love you with all my heart. Baby, I was for two days, and we spent so little time together, and I miss that. Jackie, I really want us to spend the rest of our lives together.

The first thing I said when I read this letter was boy bye. Now you thinking about us that's funny whoever your girl Kim and them? But I do feel kinda bad for him.

Josie Dennison

I'm broke, though, and I don't know my way around this town all like that, so see you when you come out dude.

Trading In My Sorrows

May 5, 2004

Dear Journal

Today I got another letter. Funny how important I really am; let's see what he has to say now.

Dear Josie,
I know I haven't been a good husband or a good father, but I really do love you and Damion. Times got hard, and I got weak, and I don't know how to be strong. But being in jail and reading the Bible I'm learning how to be strong. I am writing this to let you know that I am sorry for my behavior no matter what it takes, I'm willing to try and make things right. So I can learn to be the father and husband I am supposed to be. When I get out of jail I want to get things straight with child support so I can live my life in our home instead of jail with you and Damion. I hope you still love me and want me like you always have because without you and my kids I have no one. I'm going to commit myself to learning how to be a real man, find a job, and stay off the streets. I can't put anyone first other than God. I do not want to go out in the streets and have fun. I will stay home with my family and have fun. When you told me I should stay home that day I did not listen that's why I'm here in jail now and hurting you. From now on I'm going to hear you out because I see I have a big problem not listening to what you tell me. Sitting here gives me nothing but time to think. What I've been thinking is

Josie Dennison

since we got married I've made a lot of mistakes and I'm sorry but now I have nothing. As long as you and Damion are there, I have way more then I lost. See all I do is think about if I would have listened we would have gained more and gone further in the 2 ½ years we been together. In my whole live other than my sister that died I've never had someone to love me and care about me like you do. What I am trying to say is I've never had a real woman before you came along. That's why sometimes I act stupid. They say you never miss a good thing until it's gone or until the well runs dry. In my heart, soul, and mind I don't want to hit rock bottom to find out. So I'm asking you to forgive me because the devil is here to break up homes, and I don't want to be a victim. So in other words I'm telling you I want to get close to Jesus and raise my son in church. What I've seen happen is not where you move to or a change in scenery. The only way you are going to be happy is in Jesus Christ our Lord. That is what is going to make our marriage last and I mean this from the bottom of my heart. The reason I'm saying this to you now is because I really only talk to you like this is when I'm high. This time I'm not high, I'm for real. What I tell you here in this letter if you don't believe it or want to b=make it happen I will understand. Because I know I have told you a lot of thing I haven't done. So this time you give up and you want to let our marriage go I will understand. The only thing left would be to go back to Miami and start all over again. I'm not telling you

Trading In My Sorrows

this because this is what I want to do. I'm only saying this because I know you can only take so much.
Love Mike.

Good night Mike. Don't tell me about Jesus, and we've been married for more than 2 ½ years. You cheat so much you can't keep track.

J.

Josie Dennison

May 14, 2004

Dear Journal

Things have been going very well at the moment, but I'm not going to get too happy because every time things are going well, he'll find a way to mess it all up. I wonder why he can't just be a family man. Sad part is he thinks things are going good, so I'm waiting for the bomb to drop. How you going to be 27 years old and still hanging with teenagers? They are all about the same thing; sleeping with different women. Anyhow he ran me a bubble bath. I did feel good to finally have something nice and done for me. I enjoyed it, but I guess he really don't know me because I hate sitting in the tub. It just feels nasty. We are trying to move somewhere else, but it's not looking too good. I'll never in life trust this man. I just fell stuck cause the Jesus people gonna eat me alive if I actually leave him alone.

J.

Trading In My Sorrows

August 8, 2004

Dear Journal

I know it's been a couple of months now, but I've been busy with all this moving stuff. We're back where we started in Miami. I came home from work today and got a phone call from a girl named Summer, and yes, it was for Mike. She said she was Mike's girlfriend in Gainesville. He told her that I was his roommate. I apologized to her and told her the truth. Funny, I apologized to her for his actions cause I know lil mama was hurt. Let play a game. I think I can name them all now.

Kema
Ronny
Kim
NeNe
T. Boddy Shawn
Summer

These are just the ones I know about. I know there are more out there. I really have a messed up life. It's sad. I never had someone do me so wrong in my life, oh well. Gotta suck it up when you say "I do" or at least that's what I was told.

J.

Josie Dennison

August 26, 2004

Dear Journal

I have so many hopes and dreams. I want a nice house and a nice car, at least by the time I'm 25. But where am I doing to get those things? I'm back to where I started, and I'm depressed. On top of that, I have no motivation except for Damion. If I keep worrying about Mike, I'll really go nowhere in life. I miss my homies sometimes, but they are not thinking about me anymore. Before Mike, there was a guy that was really in love with me, but he was much older, and that scared him. I was buck wild to I wanted to hang out with my friends in school and go to prom. I was not thinking about him, so I guess this is payback. That's not really being buck wild that's wanting to be a teenager to me. I guess it depends on who you ask. But he was scared anyway.

Now I'm in pure hell, but oh well, I must deal with what I got. What in the world made me think this Mike would settle down with me of all the time to rebel? This marriage is what I should have rebelled on much harder than I did. I should have just ran. They would not have caught me until in turned 18, lol. What would they have done then? Nothing but statutory rape is a big charge, though I could not go through that lie, although I sometimes wish I would have.

J.

Trading In My Sorrows

September 1, 2004

Dear Mike

I'm having a problem, and every time I try to talk to you about it, you ignore me. Well, my problem is you. I love you, but I'm no longer in love with you. Let me break that down for you. I love you because you are my kid's father, and you take care of us, but I will not go out of my way to make you happy. The reason for this is we've been together for 3 years and were more bad times than good times. I have been trying to make things work, but every time we talk, things start going good, and you find a way to mess everything up. I have finally had enough of you and the stuff you take me through. I really, really want to just give up and say the heck with all this. But this heart of mine is telling me to give you another chance. It's hard because I know as soon as I do, you are going to trample all over me.

I'm tired of being unhappy. On my birthday I'm going to be 20 years old, and my life for as long as I can remember has been unhappy. But now I'm ready to be happy, be who I am created to be. Your money does not make me happy. I want someone who loves me and is also in love with me. I want someone who is all about me and my son. I want someone who won't cheat on me because I'm all that he wants. I thought you could be that person, but as the years went by, I see that I

Josie Dennison

was wrong. I don't know what you want to do, but I know just know I love you, but I lone myself more. My heart wants it to work, but it's just not working, and my mind knows this.

Haha, the letter I never had the guts to give him !!

J.

Trading In My Sorrows

November 8, 2004

Dear Journal

Well, my stupid dump butt is pregnant again. Why would I do this to myself? No, what should I do, work, or go to school for 9 months? Or maybe I should do both. Anyhow this is so crazy I just want to cry. How did I get pregnant by him again? Two kids by this man is not what I want at all. Now I'm really stuck; he went Christmas shopping for Damion, that's it. Guess I'm not good enough for a gift, oh well as long as my son is good, I'm good. Now I really need to save money. I'm going to cry now; good night.

J.

Josie Dennison

December 26, 2004

Dear Journal

I wish Mike would just change because I do love him very much. So much, so that can't do anything to hurt him as bad as I want to. When he's mad at me, I feel really bad, like I really messed up this time. But I tell you one thing he knows how to hurt me. I want to leave so bad. Right now, I know that would be a bad choice. He says that he loves me and that he is a changed man. I want to believe him, but I don't.

J.

Trading In My Sorrows

February 8, 2005

Dear Journal

I am six months pregnant now an all most finished with school. It's so hard for me to concentrate on what I want to do because Mike got his car back, so that means more time for his side chicks. To the back burner, I go. He was never home without the car, so it's going to be even worse now. I just want to know what I did in my life to deserve to be with this man in this mess. Am I being tested? Is this a test before the good part of my life starts? Maybe I'm being punished, but for what? I feel so stupid because my mother did not raise me to take this crap from a man, but I also keep hearing I Can't get divorced.

Every night I go to bed wondering who he's sleeping with, where he has been, and when is he going to unleash on me this time? It always comes out he rubs it in my face of all the women he's been with, and I dare not say anything. So far, three have been two added to his list; I can't remember their names. But Kim is his number one; she is all he talks about. I know he has no respect for me at all, and every time I think about it, I want to kill him. Yes, my mind has been plotting evil things. I just don't have the guts to actually do them. Sometimes I want to call the homies and have them take care of him. Sometimes I just want to kill myself

Josie Dennison

for letting a man like Mike drag me. It happens so much I don't know why it hurts so much every time I should be used to it by now. I even know when it's going to happen, but I still be hurt and be crying. Even with Damion all he did was donate some sperm because he does nothing with or for him. When I start back working, it's going to be me doing everything for my baby. Me and my stupid self went and got pregnant again. Now I'm going to be stuck with two kids while he's out with his side chicks. When he has money, he tries to hide it. I don't know what else to do except get ready because it's about to happen again, hopefully.

I won't cry this time and just deal with it. I can't tell anyone what I'm going through; not only will I look stupid, but then they will know, so I'd rather keep it to myself. The one side will tell me to leave, and those Christians will tell me that I'm not allowed to leave, so I should just stay and take it. So I'll just keep it all to myself and make sure I smile when I'm out. So ask why am I still with him; they don't understand that I'm stuck, at least for now I am. I can't even tell anyone how I feel without feeling more shame. I'm scared to make friends because he ends up sleeping with them, so I keep everyone at a safe distance. Oh well, this is my life now I'll deal with it all.

J.

Trading In My Sorrows

February 14, 2005

Dear Journal

Today is Valentine's day; as usual, I didn't get anything, not even a piece of candy. I hate this day; it's just a reminder of how much I'm not loved. Last year I was alone while he was sleeping with his A-1, and she got a nice gift. He could have at least just said happy Valentine's Day. It's the thought that counts. Maybe no one taught him that, or I just don't matter. Whatever nothing changes, it's two a.m. I know he's out with his girl. I'm just extremely depressed. I should have never listened to anyone and married this man. I should have let him just go to jail truth or lie. Maybe it's because I was so young and I was trying to do the right thing. But who cares about the right thing now. That man did not want to get married. He only did it to avoid jail; the only good thing is I got to keep Damion. I hate him so much!

J.

Josie Dennison

March 9, 2005

Dear Journal

I don't even know how to start. Yesterday a girl called for Mike; she hung up on me. He made up some lie as usual. Right after, Monique called and asked me to tell him to stop coming to her house because he is getting her in trouble. Which, to me, means they have been talking and hooking up, but today something happened that made her mad. I'm so extremely tired; I don't know what else to do. I don't even have anyone to talk to, but I can't keep letting myself go through this over and over again.

J.

Trading In My Sorrows

June 15, 2005

Dear Journal

Mike and I have been together since 2001. It is now 2005; it's like four years. That's four years of pain, suffering, and hurt. It's going on 5 a.m., and he's not home; this happens every other night sometimes; he doesn't come home at all. He's never home in the daytime. I know he's with someone else, but I don't even care anymore. I know I say that a lot, and then I end up at point -a starting all over again. Yes, it hurts, but I'm used to it by now. I feel like I'm getting punished for something that I did, but I can't think of what I did that was so bad. I had my chance to leave when he told me in Gainesville that he wanted to leave, but nope my dumb behind had to stick by him, thinking maybe he'd change, so this is what I get to be a loyal bum. That's what I get for trying to hold on to something that does not really want, so hold on to me.

J.

Josie Dennison

January 1, 2008

Dear Journal

The happiest of New Years to you, girl. What's been going on? Guess what? I know you're going to kill me. It's been so long since I've written because I was so depressed for so long. It is now New Years' though, so let's start off our new foot girl; happy 2008 to you. Let me fill you in obviously, in 3 years there's been so much going on. Guess what I got three kids now, yes, two girls and a boy Damian, Jasmine and Jessica. We are now living in Orlando. Let me tell you how we even ended up in Orlando.

I got a phone call from someone while I was at work, stating that they shot up my house. So I don't know what Mike was into, but those dudes came, and they shot up my house with my kids in it. So we basically ran to Orlando while I was big and pregnant with Jasmine. Got here, we were supposed to be staying with my sister. Come to find out that plan was a no-go, so we ended up staying with one of her friends, which was very random. We stayed until we got our apartment. Wow, while living in this apartment, so much drama happened. It doesn't even make sense that this man can get involved in so much and such a short time. Mind you, we moved here in 2005, going in 2006. I ended up having my baby girl here in Orlando. I was so stressed out because I was again pregnant by the same man. My baby came out at 4 lbs., and born at five or six months. I don't know for sure because I didn't seek medical treatment, thinking that would make baby girls disappear or something. I don't know what I was thinking. The day I went to the hospital, I felt really bad because it was on my son's birthday, so I really didn't celebrate him that year. You should have seen the look on his face when I told him his gift was a little sister. He was like, what am I going to do with that.

I was surprised she was so healthy and shocked; she was my skin color dark. That made me happy I did not abort her. But Mike's mom convinced him that he needed to do a blood test because he's never had a dark-skinned child. That how you know I'm in a bunch of idiots, how I'm dark as night, but you don't think I can have a dark skin child. Plus, he's the one always running around sleeping with everyone. I'm not even allowed to leave the house without him. So, where did I sleep with someone on top of the counter at work? I guess. It bothered me at first, but then I realized the people I was dealing with go ahead and do your baddest. My baby girl is here and healthy.

Anyhow, he started selling drugs with these country bumpkins, and I try to explain to this dude that these country dudes up here are not like the dudes he deals within Miami. And sure enough, they ended up robbing us

Josie Dennison

because of the medallion around Damion's neck. So that the past, and right after this whole drama of getting robbed, we end up moving to a house in Ocala. I made some Mormon friends along the way. They started coming around when we were in the apartment, and they continue trying to teach us the word and trying to get us to come to church. I got baptized while I was pregnant with baby girl, but I don't want anything to do with Church at this point in life. Do say nothing about going to church and all that to me. I know God exists, just not for me; he's more interested in those fake hypocrite people of his. Back to the house, funny how we end up moving to this house, and it's a very nice house, but it was a struggle to get the house; it was even more struggle to keep the house.

My Mormon friend helped us get the house. Our home teacher signed as a reference on the house for us. I was shocked because he knew everything that was going on in my life, but he and his wife felt the need to help us. Mike keeps trying to convince me to use them and ask them for money, but I refuse to. These people have been so good to us. The only real Godly people I've seen. This is when I found out that Mike had been doing drugs, he had become his own best customer, and we're not talking about some weed. Instead of taking that help that these Mormon people have for us, he tried to pimp them; thank God they caught on. But I would say my home teacher or whatever they call

Trading In My Sorrows

themselves is a great man. He would come to my house to teach me the word he taught me how to drive secretly. Yes, he taught me how to drive I secret because Mike would catch a fit if he knew that I know how to drive. I haven't told anyone yet, but this thing with Mike started getting worse, especially with the dragging me around and stuff. When my home teacher is here, though, Mike won't touch me. I love it when he comes, and I ask all the questions in the world because, for a moment, I am safe. Right before we left Miami, this dude dragged me by my hair through the parking lot because he thought that I snitched about something that was going on. I had no idea about anything; the cops just came knocking on our door. Now that we are here in Orlando, you would think things would change but nope.

Things have gotten worst; this is as bad as it's ever been. Last Christmas, I brought the kids all kinds of gifts and had to return each and every last one of them because this dude smoked up our light bill and money our rent money. I gave this dude my food stamp card to go buy some groceries. When I came home, granted the house was full of food, I asked him why he got all packaged chicken that was already cooked; this stuff has to be super expensive. You know my little nosey self was playing detective trying to figure out what he did to get all this expensive food that's already cooked, and he couldn't provide any receipts. So then a few days

Josie Dennison

later, someone comes knocking and talking about my card declined. So I asked them why they would know anything about my card. Come to find out, he sold the food stamps and got the food from the baked part of the grocery store; the food that they were getting ready to throw away, he asked them to give it all to him. So the question now is what happened to my stamps. This person wants their money back. The people filled someone else house with food, which is why I started going to the store with him. This is just some of the things that I've been dealing with, which is why I haven't been writing. I've been super overwhelmed, trying to keep my life together.

Finally, we got kicked out of that house in Ocala because Mike called himself trying to light a bonfire, and it burned the siding of the house, so guess who had to replace that? I did. I'm just so over this. My Mormon friends finally couldn't take anymore, so he just stopped coming around, and I can't blame them. Mike started going off on them because I started going to their church. I was only going to get away from Mike.

Their church is really different; they separated everyone for teaching, but they did not call it Sunday school they would teach us about different things in life.
Then we would get back together for the big service. It was okay, but I was afraid of what they were teaching my kids and why I can't go in the kids' room.

Trading In My Sorrows

Were they preparing them to take over the world? Then the church part, they only played soft, creepy music. I asked why they said because Jesus is soft or something like that. Well, they got tired of coming around. Mike was abusing them, and I had too many questions, I guess. I must say, though, when it comes to helping, those people will help anyone in need, and they are not afraid to step into any situation. They really trust in their god and Joseph Smith's teaching. Every time I think of how Mike treated them, I feel bad, and they were only trying to help me out. If I make it out of this situation, I hope I can find them and tell them thank you. I'll never forget them even if I don't understand what they were talking about half the time, and their military church service is kinda of weird.

I tried to apply for another apartment to move to. They told me that I owed the old apartment. From what I recalled, I paid for one of those and made sure they were paid. I couldn't figure out what they were talking about if it was some security deposit or whatever, so I called the apartments to see what I owe them. And she gave me the date that I moved out, and I was like,

"Hold on because I moved out way before that I gave the papers in and everything."

Josie Dennison

So guess what this dude did? He never gave him the papers the whole time we were living in that house in Ocala. He had some girl that he was messing with, and her mom moves into the old apartment under my name, isn't that lovely. Because of this, as of right now, we are living in a hotel that was converted into some type of apartment. We have to pay weekly. We pay more to live in this hotel room than to stay and a regular apartment with our three kids. I'll say this again; I am so over this. I have to start making plans. It's to the point where he knows I want to go, and he knows that I'm making my way to leave, and whenever he gets like a sense that I'm ready to go, he'll clean up his ass and make all kinds of stupid promises.

J.

Trading In My Sorrows

March 26, 2008

Dear Journal

So we've been staying at this hotel since February it's not that bad. I just really want to stay in a regular apartment with my kids. And as far as for Mike and me goes, I guess things are okay. I don't know how okay they can be living in a hotel, but I'm trying to make the best of it. And even in this situation, I'm sure he'll find a way to mess things up. I started back talking to my sister, but I had to stop because he claimed that she would call the child protective services on us, so stop talking to her. He had me try this blue pill, and it had some type of stamp on it. I promise you I thought I was going to die; my heart was racing; I couldn't sit still. I was drinking so much water, and I kept looking over my shoulder as if somebody was out to get me. Later on, I found out it was ecstasy. I promise you this dude does anything to try to get me hooked on drugs so that I don't see or focus on the things that he's doing, no sir.

J.

Josie Dennison

August 18, 2008

Dear Journal

I'm back in Miami again; yes, I know another move. We've been back for a month now, and we really don't want to be back. Orlando is so much better. I feel like yep, this was another mistake, but hey, I keep telling myself, "We're young, and we're still trying to find our place in life."

I really want to go back, but at the same time, I don't want to move again. I just want to be a stay-at-home with me and my family. I think this is God's way of telling Mike and I, just slow down and pay attention. Okay people around us and who's really trying to help us out. So the plan is to get my place to get the kids enrolled in school how to get myself enrolled in school. I really want to stay out of everyone's face because everyone is so fake, but it's okay. I can deal. Mike and I stopped talking to this one girl that I had been talking to for a while. I came back to Miami and found out she had been running her mouth to Mike's brother-in-law well, little did she know they came and told us everything that was said. I'm back now, so what's up.

Trading In My Sorrows

I'm just so ready to get out of here. I'll just be in a Hole by myself with my kids; these people are so dramatic they turn everything that's not their business into their business and spread rumors and lies. Coming back was the worst mistake of my life.
Maybe on the bright side, God is trying to teach us how to be strong together and depend on each other if he even sees us.

J.

Josie Dennison

September 1, 2008

Dear Journal

As of right now, I feel like a star. I'm the topic at everyone's table. You can't go a day without thinking or simply talking about me, hahaha yes me I'm always on the front of your mind even if I don't know you. Why do so many people envy me? Well, why not? She's 23 years old and has done what they're still trying to do. When she falls, everyone who loves it, but when she comes back, watch out! Now double the strength double portion stronger than before, which brings more envy.

They ask themselves why Mike chose her, but why not look at her-yeah. I've been trying to take him and sleep with him and do nasty things with him; however, he still comes back. They want this man so bad, but yet, they don't know what I had to go through, and I'm still going through with this man. If anything, as soon as I get back on my feet, come take them. While you're at it, do all the necessary work to keep them stop sending him back

J.

Trading In My Sorrows

September 12, 2008

Dear Journal

Last night I had the biggest breakdown that I could possibly think of. I was yelling and screaming about why my life ended up this way, why are we in this position that we are in. I think that was my weakest point up to now. This has to be a wake-up call either for me or for the both of us.

I talked to Mike about all the decisions that I wanted, and basically, what I said was I just want to give it all up like I'm just done. This lifestyle has gotten way out of hand. I'm just over it all, and I can't take anymore. He claimed we would work on it together and seek some type of counseling until we got things right.

I figured that was a good plan; it was better than what I had planned, which is to send my kids to my mother and just commit suicide. That's the easy way out, though. The other option would be to give my life over to Jesus Christ and let him fix it; that's not happening either. So we'll see where we go from here.

J.

Josie Dennison

November 4, 2008

Dear Journal

Last night a change was made. Mr. Barack Obama was elected as president of the United States; yes, Journal, a black man is the President of the United States; how awesome is that. Just watching that is a motivation all these changes being made that just means if he can do it, so can I. All I have to do is stay focused and get my life right and stop talking about this suicidal stuff. That just means that my son even has a chance to become something in life; he doesn't have to be like these people he's surrounded by. The real question is, how in the world am I going to do that. President Barack Obama, the first black man elected as president of the United States, I am so.

J.

Trading In My Sorrows

February 20, 2009

Dear Journal

I guess we're back to living on top of the world again. I'm not sure I like it up here; it's not what it's cracked up to be. So we're renting a house in Hollywood, Florida from my boss, and it's a really nice house, it's really big. I hardly ever see the kids because they're on the other side of the house; it has a sunroof so you can see outside; it's really nice. But for some reason, Mike thinks that we can throw parties here every other night because we have so much space.

I don't think he realizes that this is my boss's house, so we can't be tearing things up; we don't own the place we're just renting. And these parties just end up making people hate us more because they're thinking that oh, we're living the high life when in reality, I'm getting molly-whopped every night. These parties ain't no little parties. I'm talking about heavy drug use and heavy drinking. The good thing is I have my drinks as long as I get my drink on; I'm good; whatever can happen just give me my E&J. Only found something that I love more than a man E & J Easy Jezzy.

J.

Josie Dennison

March 3, 2009

Dear Journal

Okay, now I think I have a problem. I had to be at work early in the morning, and I went in there so drunk that you can smell the alcohol coming out of my port; however, I was able to do my job and function right; of course, my boss pulled me to the side and was like no ma'am. So I have to find a better way to hide this. As long as I can function, I think I'm good; they sell this little flask that you can put on a belt or like these cups that people can't see what's inside your cup. I think I'm going to invest in one of those because I need my E&J.

J.

Trading In My Sorrows

October 20, 2009

Dear Journal

Well, last night was another bad night. I don't want this to go. This is the worst break put in history. Mike raped me last night. If I could kill him, I would have last night. Do you know how it feels to have your clothes ripped off you and this person you hate forcing himself on top of you? I yelled and tried to fight him off till I finally just gave up and let it happen. Whatever, who's going to believe me anyway, my husband rapped me. Every day he makes the situation worst with the things he says and the things he does. On top of that, he erased all my contacts and changed my phone number.

J.

Josie Dennison

October 23, 2009

Dear Journal

So Mike's cousin and sister were having a party, and he told me to come so I can drive Mike home after so I did. Well, after I got there and kinda stayed to myself. When it was time to go, Mike refused to let me drive said his plan was to kill us all. This fool got on the highway doing 100 in the opposite direction of traffic. When too many cars were coming, this dude jumped out of the car and left me and the kids. The car ran through a brick wall into a warehouse. I was so scared the kids peed all over themselves; my dress was ripped from fighting with Mike, so I was practically naked.

Thank God there were cameras, so some guys from inside the warehouse came out to help us and call the cops. Cops brought us home, and Damion would not go inside; he was scared that night. My son said to me, "Mom, if we don't leave we are going to die," I knew that was it times to go. So here we go making plans to leave for good this time.

J.

Trading In My Sorrows

November 23, 2009

Dear Journal

This may be the longest entry yet because it's the beginning of my new life; Girl, sit back and listen. I don't know if I told you before, but we were living in Hollywood, Florida, and Mike hit a big score doing some grimy stuff, and we were living nice, but nothing had changed. So I finally worked us the strength to leave Mike after almost 10 years of abuse. So check this out how this happened.

We already had everything planned; we would go our separate ways. Then he started switching up, but this time I was too done. I decided to drive myself to work, and after I would go to the nail salon. I came home a little later than usual, and this dude went made. He beat the crap out of me, but he didn't realize that I gained some extra know-how all this time of fighting him. I got with him. Finally, he went and got some pills and tried to force me to take the pills with him to kill ourselves. He took them, but I did not. I tried to leave the house, but this dude locked the doors from the outside.

Well, in the morning, I lied and said I was going to work, but he told me to go ask the neighbors for a ride because he cut the brake lines to my car. I went next

Josie Dennison

door to my racist neighbor asking for help, though they have called to cops on us many nights to fight. But the woman was nice to me, begging me to leave. I told her

I was ready. Well, while sitting there, I decided I would pay to the God I gave up on years ago. It was a really short prayer;

"God, I'm ready to go from here. I don't know how but I'll leave everything behind if you just give me my kids. I'll go and try to live for you.

Girl, why the kids come walking over? That old man threw us in the car and took off. We went to the police station. The cop told me if I should just leave quietly she'll make a report for me to cover me. Funny thing is she had been to my house plenty, so she knew exactly who I was and what I was going through. In fact she was the same cop that removed me from the house on A-Stay way order the one time I beat the crap out of Mike. We rode around the city for a while cause I didn't have any family in Miami. While I was making plans, I was able to get in contact with my siblings. All had relocated halfway across the world.

So I called his sister asked for help knowing she was not too fond of me. Well, she let us come and live in her basement for a little while as I try to figure out my next move. Well, Mikes' oldest son found us. I asked him

Trading In My Sorrows

not to tell his dad. Well, he didn't rat me out; instead, he started sneaking me my personal items from the house. One of my bosses got me a train ticket and transferred my job on the condition that I would never come back. I got in touch with my siblings again and told them I was coming up. I'm sure they did not believe me cause many times I had said I was coming up but never did. Well, little did they know things had gotten so bad that Mike did not like me even talking to them.

So anyhow, I had to spend about 1 week down there waiting for my train departure date. Mike came over almost every day and never knew I was down there. I literally had to hold the girls' mouth shut sometimes to make sure they did not say a word. I had no problem with the boy. When it was time for me to go, the ladies from my job had packed up some stuff for me, and my one boss got the kids and me some clothes, food, and everything we needed to go. We had no clue where we were going; I just know all my siblings and mom went up there. She went with me to the train station because I was so scared. I knew for sure he would be waiting to kill us. Well, nope, he wasn't there, and she made sure we got o that train safe.

J.

Josie Dennison

November 4, 2009

Dear Journal

Here I am in New Jersey with a 5-hour layover. I don't even know what that means or where I'm at I'm literally just sitting here. The baby ran out of diapers, so I rapped that brown hand drying paper towel around her butt; hopefully, that will hold. They are all hungry, and I have no money, so I sent the boy to McDonald's to ask if they could please give them some food. I can't get up and ask myself cause the baby peed all over me in socked with pee.

I've been crying all night; I don't want to do this no more. Maybe Mike was right. I don't know how to take care of 3 kids. We had nannies at one point, so I really don't know somethings. I don't even know my own clothes size. Cause Mike brought all my clothes for me, he didn't like me going into the stores to shop. I really just want to call my squad family and have them come get me. I can apologize to my kids later and explain to them I tried to live the lifestyle but could not and just pray they understand. Oh, wait, I think they are calling for us to get back on the train; OMG, I don't want to get lost. I'm so scared I don't know what I am doing.

J.

Trading In My Sorrows

November 6, 2009

Dear Journal

I'm sitting here and praying for this God who took me out of the situation to show me what's next; then, out of nowhere, I felt something next to me, but I didn't care. I just wanted to cry and go back home. How I even know that this so-called God that left me hanging is real? I go somewhere I don't even want to be around people who don't even know me even though we shared the same blood. At this point, I don't even care what about these people. Jesus people have to say about me or my kids, I'll pop someone in the mouth if I have too. Anit nothing I'll go back where I came from.

J.

Josie Dennison

November 27, 2009

Dear Journal

I'm here only because my boss got me a one-way ticket and I'm broke. My siblings came and got me; I'm at my mom's house, feeling like what. I thought I need to find a shelter in the world, but they were all full. My lil brother and sister are actually kinda cool. They have been trying to get me to read the Bible and go to church (someone says major eye roll.) I don't even understand what this book is talking about, like the Jack in the Bean Stock language. Who wrote this stuff? I just try my best to stay to myself until I get out of here. I need my own place—this church stuff is for the birds. Me and Mom are still the same stay over there, and I'll be out your way really soon. Deep down, I know she don't want me in her house, which is cool cause I don't want to be here either. Trust me, the first chance I get, I'm out.

J.

Trading In My Sorrows

December 8, 2009

Dear Journal

It's been a while since I wrote in you. I've been so busy getting things in order for the kids and school and all that. Well, I've been working good. My boss really did transfer my job for me. I've been doing the church thing; the pastor is really cool. He ain't one of those I've never did wrong type dudes. He told the whole world that he use to do drugs. I'm shocked my mom comes to this church under an ex addicted lol. It is what it is, though; I like him. I already had it out with one of the members; she was asking for a molly woop. God almost answered her prayers that Sunday (lol). I got her number, though. I bet she won't say nothing else to me. She went snitching to the pastor; what he gonna do? Only Jesus can save you right now. Next time you see me, you better just shut up and worship.

J.

Josie Dennison

January 10, 2010

Dear Journal

Well, guess what happened today? There is this old white lady at the church always crying to pray with me, so I started running from her when I see her coming. I even asked her nicely to please leave me be I can pray for myself. I think she's deaf, or she just don't care. Well, today, I didn't run fast enough. She laid hands on me. I refused to pray, so I just stood there, eye closed, rolling my eyes on the inside, trying to be nice. Then my stomach started burning, and before I knew it, I was on the floor. I was yelling and crying and slobbering all over the place; thank God I had pants on. I don't know what kinda colt mess they got going on, like that dude on TV throwing people on the floor with his jacket. If she wasn't so old, I would believe she threw me on the floor, but I know it was God. Once I got up, she was like;

"You got the Holy Ghost honey praise, God."
I just rolled my eye at her and gave her a hug anyway. Maybe now she will leave me alone, lol. I can't do this every week.

J.

Trading In My Sorrows

February 5, 2010

Dear Journal

Girl, I'm making new friends of my own this is amazing. They offered me to come have a drink with them as much as I would love to; they don't know that one drink can make me go backwards. I'm the best drinker there is, haha, so I just be saying no thank I'm trying to do this Jesus thing. Well, remember a few months ago I was running from the old lady why she and I are friends now (lol) she told me I need to get baptized I was like, here we go. I was baptized at the Morman church. She was like;
"No honey, you need to be baptized in Jesus' name."
I'm like, Fine Lady, since you probably visit him every night, I think he's talking to you. (lol.) Syck naw.

J.

Josie Dennison

April 30, 2010

Dear Journal

It's been a long, long time. Well, let me fill you in, Girl. I did end up getting baptized in the name of Jesus, and my brother got me a Bible. I understand it's called the NLT. I call it the street translation, but yeah. I've been doing my own studying. I literally had to erase everything I was taught as a child and start fresh. Man, did they tell me lies.

I found out that Jesus actually loves me, and no matter what I've done in the past, he washed all that away. Now I understand why this old lady was in me so hard. I call her Old Lady but trust me, by now, I know her name very well.

I got my own first apartment; we are sleeping on blow-up beds, but it's my floor, and no one can say anything to me. I got a car; it's a lemon, but it's my lemon, and I renamed her Lexus; at least that's what I feel lie when I'm driving. People laugh we I say I drive a KIA, but her name is Lexus; honey, if only they knew.

I've learned how to pray. I've been doing a lot of it too. And they all get answered in a wired way. Let me give you an example I pray for God to help me buy school clothes for my kids. Then right after, my car got hit by

Trading In My Sorrows

some old lady. I didn't know anything about how insurance worked; they have my money for the damages. Well the shops said:

"Buy a new car; this one is not worth fixing," I didn't need a car; mine ran just fine, so the money furnished my apartment and covered school. To think I didn't even see the lady hit my car. I was inside working, thank God my brother caught it. But that's the type of stuff that's been happening, and this Holy Spirit has been helping me fight so many different things it's amazing. I gotta have more cause I haven't even wanted to drink since I got it.

I want to start a ladies' support group to help women coming out of situations like me. I'm not sure how I will do it or when, but I know this is God cause I don't mess around with this helping people stuff, but whatever I promised him, I would serve him, so gotta keep that promise. The only thing is now I actually want to do it. He's making me soft (lol). God is actually going to use everything I've been through for good. I can't wait to see how my life will turn out.

Oh, and by the way, this is my last Dear Journal. I'm transitioning to Dear God; he said he's my friend that's always there, so I'm going to try and count on that. I'm so enjoying this life too; I guess cause I was in a bad relationship but in due time though, God has to fix me first. I guess I'll be bust for a minute, but I have to

Josie Dennison

leave you with some stuff I wrote. I was digging deep, I guess.

J.

Trading In My Sorrows

NOT A FOOL

Knowing that he's the one who brought me through

What a fool I would be to not praise his name.

What a fool I would be to not

Lift his name up high.

What a fool I would be to not do a simple task as to try best

To follow his path and walk in his glory.

What a fool I would be to not

Acknowledge him when he speaks.

Me, be a fool, why?

To give up my chance at eternal life walking in his light.

I think NOT.

Josie Dennison

February 1, 2011

Dear God

Today, when I dropped the kids off at school, it was nice to see how they looked so happy and clean. Then after class, I was feeling kinda down cause I thought that I failed my math class, but God is good. I'll keep hope alive and stick in there till the end. Then after class, I so badly wanted a soda, but the thought of bread also crossed my mind because i don't have any rice. I went to the store and spent my last $3.80 on a loaf of bread and a small Pepsi.

Something inside of me wanted to feel depressed, being that I work so hard, and that's all I could afford. But then reality hit me, and I remembered my problems 2 years ago. A strung-out husband, fighting every night, drinking problems, always on the run and kids with no direction, and no God in my life.

So I praise God I've been made new, and I praise for all He has taken me through in order to learn the things I do know now. The roads are hard; however, they were even harder before I accepted Jesus into my life. Now, whenever I go through something, I see it as a test, a

Trading In My Sorrows

lesson, or the ways of the world playing mind games with me.

J.

Josie Dennison

February 14, 2011

WHAT'S THE MEANING OF LOVE?

LOVE IS I WANT YOU TO COME OVER JUST SO YOU CAN NEXT TO ME.

LOVE IS I'LL PICK A FIGHT WITH YOU JUST FOR YOUR ATTENTION.

LOVE IS I HATE YOU RIGHT NOW, BUT YOU BETTER REMEMBER I LOVE YOU.

LOVE IS I'LL GIVE YOU MY LAST, ALTHOUGH IT'S GOING TO HURT ME, IT'S WORTH SEEING THE JOY IT BRINGS YOU.

LOVE IS I'M IGNORING YOU RIGHT NOW BECAUSE I'D RATHER NOT TELL YOU I DON'T LIKE WHAT YOU'RE DOING.

LOVE IS A SMILE UPON MY FACE WHEN I THINK OF YOU BECAUSE WE JUST HAD AN ARGUMENT.

LOVE IS ME RUNNING TO YOUR EVERY CALL.

LOVE IS MY HEART CRUSHING WHEN OTHERS DO YOU WRONG.

Trading In My Sorrows

LOVE IS LENDING MY SHOULDER FOR YOU TO VENT ON.

LOVE IS NEVER JUGDEING YOU BASED ON YOUR FLAWS.

LOVE IS IN MY EYES YOU CAN DO NO WRONG.

J.

Josie Dennison

HOW GREAT IS OUR GOD

My God is so good to me. Looking back at my life, I remember many nights I would cry myself to sleep because of the things in my life, my surroundings, my husband, and so forth. Words can't even explain the feeling I bare inside. The way my life is going now, I use to daydream about back then. I been born again. I'm with my family; I attend college, I have a great job, my kids are oh so blessed, my friends are all positive people.

As I write this page, I help but to let the tears flow. I praise God for all that he's done for me. My sleepless night is now because of homework or thoughts of how great my God is to me, no longer up crying due to the beating my husband just gave me. I can now play in the park with my kids; no one telling me that they don't have time for that.

I take great pleasure in our morning routine full of love, no more waking up at 2pm. We sit in my room watch a movie as they share their ideas with me; no more kids stay on your side of the house. I can drive to and from as I please; no more waiting for him to take me when he felt like it. I can see my family (especially my little sister, brother, mother, and grandmother) as I please; no more promises of visits that die because he feels as if we have more important things to do. I attend the house of God as I should; no more crying, hoping, and wishing. I attend school, no more putting it off. I pay all my bills, no more going without. My kids are free to be; no more stuck in the room because of him and his company.

I've asked for things in the past that were put off or just not important enough to look into; I now have at my leisure. My kids have excelled so much. They're able to use their minds to the fullest, and in by the blood of Jesus, they will continue to do so. My God is so great. My nights of silent prayers from back then, God has answered them all. My dreams are being fulfilled thanks to God and his great merciful

Josie Dennison

March 17, 2011

THINGS SEEN THROUGH MY EYES

Why is it so hard for us as people to just stop and think of others feeling before we do and say things.

Sometimes I feel like I put too much of myself out there in ways that no one could possibly understand.

Therefore, it seems like any little thing hurts.

What am I to do when the little things are what I clang to?

Things that mean so much to me mean absolutely nothing too you

I know I'm cut differently to the opposing view.

You never see me, yet I can't get rid of you.

But never the less, No matter what people say, think or do I shall remain strong until my date is due.

Trading In My Sorrows

April 20, 2011

Dear Journal,

Come closer let me whisper something to you.
"I have a secret."

A promise from my father and I'm clinging to it."

So yes, I'm cut differently, but I'm fine with it.

You may not have noticed because you're not focused.

It's painfully obvious your poundings, picking, and kicking may hurt me.

But you will never reach the one that dwells within me.

I take it to Him; then He puts you to an end.

The man God sends has been shaped and molded.

His pride will be for the others like you and worldly things you drag with you.

Josie Dennison

His feeling he will share not to despair the positive aroma he brings to my atmosphere. Miles mean nothing to him if it makes me smile.

The time we spend will be precious to him, for I'm the river that flows down his mountain.
He will love my offspring as if they were his own

His desires will be to seek God first in everything, not just when it hurts.

The bond we share together, as one can only be topped by the only begotten son

In reflection to Pauls' letter in my own words: Colossians 1

On January 10, 2010, I accepted the good news.

I was baptized in the name of Jesus, also received the baptism of the Holy ghosts.

The secret about Christ was then revealed to me.

Ever since then, I've been pressing and building my relationship with God a.k.a Jesus Christ.

In Colossians 2, Paul says: Let your roots grow down into him, and let your lives be built on him. Then your faith

Trading In My Sorrows

will grow strong in the truth you were taught, and you will overflow with thankfulness.

As I pray daily, I take in the teachings and try my best to self-apply everything that I take in. I ask questions seeking knowledge about the things that I don't understand and reading the word as often as I can. I bare witness that the deeper one plants themself into the Lord our God, making him the center of all things, even the little things you gain new eyes that will build a new heart meaning new love.

J.

Josie Dennison

With New Eyes

You can see outside the box, no longer seeing things the way you use too.

With a new heart

You will start to love the things of God, casting away desires of the heart before God.

With new love

A softened and humble heart that cares, cries, and knows that there's more than what the world sees.

Trading In My Sorrows

Dear Journal

May 3rd 2011

When I first came here, I got a restraining order in Florida. I got a stay-away order from my current location for him not to even come in the same state. I didn't even think that was possible, but you'll be surprised what a sympathetic judge can do. The only thing with that order is I can't get child support because Mike's not allowed to visit his children, which is fine with me. God got us. I talked to my pastor one day, and he counseled me on divorce, and the only reason that I'd be able to file. This counseling took months, but he helped me understand, and with that, I went and filed. Mike didn't know that this is a commonwealth or common law state; therefore, he doesn't have to be around for me to file for divorce; I don't even need his signature. I just need to post an ad in the paper locally, and in the paper, in the state that he resides, checkmate Mike it's done. I'm enjoying this walking in this new life, ready for new things to come. I'm not sure where God is going to take me from here on, but I'm sure about being ready to go. I know it's been on my heart to do this ladies ministry thing, but before I can help others, I need to focus on getting myself right especially right with God. I know I did him wrong for many years. The pastor recently preached a sermon about trading sorrows for joy and all this other stuff, not sure how I'm going to do it

Josie Dennison

because it is hard letting everything go and moving on, but I'm trying every day. Plus, I be so busy trying to get this new life right I don't even have time to think about the old life, but I guess I just can't let it down without actually digging into me first. I still cry every night; however,

    I'm not crying because someone cheated on me or beat me or anything like that. I'm crying because I'm no longer in that situation, but what took me so long to get out, and why is it that my son had to open my eyes, or maybe god used him to do it. So these are more likely tears for joy.

J.

Trading In My Sorrows

www.ingramcontent.com/pod-product-compliance
Lightning Source LLC
Chambersburg PA
CBHW060202050426
42446CB00013B/2949